DISCARD

BLOOMINGTON PUBLIC LIBRARY

S0-ARL-501

A11905 996199

BLOOMINGTON PUBLIC LIBRARY

205 E. OLIVE STREET

POST OFFICE BOX 3308

BLOOMINGTON, ILLINOIS 61701

BLOOMINGTON, ILLINOIS
PUBLIC LIBRARY

St. Patrick's Day

by Natalie M. Rosinsky

Content Adviser: Dr. Alexa Sandmann, Professor of Literacy,
The University of Toledo; Member, National Council for the Social Studies

Reading Adviser: Dr. Linda D. Labbo, Department of Reading Education,
College of Education, The University of Georgia

Let's See Library
Compass Point Books
Minneapolis, Minnesota

J
HOL
394.262
ROS

Compass Point Books
3722 West 50th Street, #115
Minneapolis, MN 55410

Visit Compass Point Books on the Internet at *www.compasspointbooks.com* or e-mail your
request to *custserv@compasspointbooks.com*

Cover: Stained glass window of St. Patrick in Clogheen Church, County Tipperary, Ireland

Photographs ©: Richard Cummins, cover, 8, 14, 16; Unicorn Stock Photos/Jean Higgins, 4; Hulton/Archive by
Getty Images, 6, 10; Reuters/Mark Cardwell/Hulton/Archive by Getty Images, 12; Skjold Photography, 18; Reuters
NewMedia Inc./Corbis, 20; John Cross/The Free Press, 24.

Editor: Catherine Neitge
Photo Researcher: Svetlana Zhurkina
Photo Selector: Catherine Neitge
Designer: Melissa Voda

Library of Congress Cataloging-in-Publication Data
Rosinsky, Natalie M. (Natalie Myra)
    Saint Patrick's Day / by Natalie M. Rosinsky; reading adviser, Linda D. Labbo.
        v. cm.— (Let's see library)
    Includes bibliographical references and index.
    Contents: What is Saint Patrick's Day? — Who was Saint Patrick? — What did Saint Patrick really do? —
How did Saint Patrick's Day begin? —What are Saint Patrick's Day parades? — How else is Saint Patrick's Day
observed? — How has Saint Patrick's Day changed? — How is Saint Patrick's Day observed in the United
States? — How is Saint Patrick's Day observed in Ireland?
        ISBN 0-7565-0394-9 (hardcover)
        1. Saint Patrick's Day—Juvenile literature. [1. Saint Patrick's Day. 2. Holidays.] I. Title. II. Series.
    GT4995.P3 R67 2002
    394.262—dc21   2002003045

© 2003 by Compass Point Books
All rights reserved. No part of this book may be reproduced without written permission from the publisher. The publisher
takes no responsibility for the use of any of the materials or methods described in this book, nor for the products thereof.
Printed in the United States of America.

Table of Contents

What Is Saint Patrick's Day?

Saint Patrick's Day is a holiday with many roots. It is part of the **Roman Catholic** religion. Saint Patrick's Day is also part of the history of Ireland. This history began centuries before any Irish people were **Christian.**

March 17 is said to be the day on which Saint Patrick died in about the year 460. Every March 17, people in Ireland and Irish-Americans observe Saint Patrick's Day. But someone does not have to be Roman Catholic or Irish to join in the fun!

◄ *Saint Patrick's Day is tied to the history of Ireland.*

Who Was Saint Patrick?

Patrick was born in the country now called Scotland. His wealthy father was a Roman official. Their family was Christian, but the young Patrick gave little thought to his faith.

Around the year 401, Patrick was carried off by bandits. He was taken to Ireland. Patrick slaved there for six years. Patrick believed he had been a bad Christian, but he found comfort in prayer. We know Patrick's thoughts from a book he later wrote.

Patrick escaped. He became a priest. Patrick returned to Ireland to teach Christianity.

◄ *Saint Patrick taught the Irish about Christianity.*

What Did Saint Patrick Really Do?

Patrick led many Irish people to become Christian. He earned their trust by respecting their old ways. For example, they had welcomed spring with bonfires. Patrick included bonfires in the **Celtic** observance of Easter each spring. They had prayed to the sun. Patrick added the Celtic sign for the sun to the Christian cross. Christian churches became centers of learning.

Patrick became famous. Stories spread about his supposed powers. One of these **legends** is that he drove all the snakes out of Ireland!

◄ *Celtic crosses in County Sligo, Ireland*

How Did Saint Patrick's Day Begin?

Saint Patrick's Day began as a Christian holiday. Even before Patrick was named the **patron saint** of Ireland, its people loved him. They attended church on March 17. Irish people wore bits of **shamrock** on that day. It was said that Patrick had used this plant to teach Christianity.

Over time, people followed churchgoing with visits, singing, and dancing.

In the twelfth century, Ireland began a long struggle. Many people wanted independence from England. Saint Patrick's Day became a time to show pride in the Irish nation and spirit.

◄ A girl holds shamrocks in this old drawing.

What Are Saint Patrick's Day Parades?

Parades have been part of Saint Patrick's Day for hundreds of years. Irish soldiers serving in the English army paraded through New York City in 1762. Today, more than 120 cities in the United States have Saint Patrick's Day parades. The biggest ones are in New York City and Chicago.

People march to Irish music, wear shamrocks, and carry real or toy **shillelaghs**. Some people show pride in their Irish background by the "wearing of the green." Others wear green to show their friendship for Ireland and their love of fun.

◀ *Bagpipers march past Saint Patrick's Cathedral in New York City's Saint Patrick's Day parade.*

How Else Is Saint Patrick's Day Observed?

At parades, people may wave the green, white, and orange flag of Ireland. Sometimes, people carry a green banner decorated with a gold harp. Irish history and legends were once sung to the music of **harps**.

Feasts of Irish foods are also part of this special day. Corned beef and cabbage and soda bread are often eaten. Sometimes, cakes, cookies, and even drinks are colored green!

People may decorate their homes or clothing just for Saint Patrick's Day. Shamrocks and pictures of the Irish elf called a leprechaun are favorites.

◄ *A signpost in County Kerry, Ireland*

How Has Saint Patrick's Day Changed?

Observing Saint Patrick's Day was once against the law. In the 1500s, the English king made all such Roman Catholic beliefs illegal. In the 1800s, English soldiers were not allowed to wear shamrocks. These Saint Patrick's Day signs supported Irish independence. The English rulers feared losing power over Ireland.

Even in the United States, Saint Patrick's Day observances were not always welcome. Many Irish people moved here in the 1800s. Some people then disliked the Irish. They shouted and threw things at people marching in Saint Patrick's Day parades.

◄ *A statue in County Cork, Ireland, represents the many Irish who left their country and moved to the United States.*

How Is the Day Observed in the United States?

Most Irish-Americans observe Saint Patrick's Day. Many other people also join in the fun. School bands enjoy marching in the parades. City leaders and employees sometimes march.

Saint Patrick's Day is not a national holiday. Schools, businesses, and government offices are open. However, many people watch the parades, "wear the green," or eat foods dyed green.

In schools, children sometimes make Saint Patrick's Day decorations. Many children wear green clothes to school.

◄ *The "wearing of the green" is common on Saint Patrick's Day.*

How Is the Day Observed in Ireland?

Saint Patrick's Day is a national holiday in Ireland. Schools, businesses, and government offices are closed. Many people attend church. In the afternoon, children may act in plays about Saint Patrick. They may sing Irish songs or play Irish music. Friends and family gather.

In the past, parades were a small part of this holiday in Ireland. The city of Dublin has changed this. Its Saint Patrick's Day parade is now part of activities that last four full days!

◄ *A child waves the Irish flag during Dublin's Saint Patrick's Day parade.*

Glossary

Celtic—name of the people in ancient Ireland and of the language they spoke

Christian—a member of the faith that believes Jesus Christ is the son of God

harp—a stringed musical instrument

legend—tall tale told about a real person

patron saint—a holy person who helps others

Roman Catholic—a branch of the Christian religion

shamrock—a leaf with three parts, like clover

shillelagh—a short, heavy club

Did You Know?

• Two grand churches are named for the Irish patron saint. These are Saint Patrick's Cathedral in New York City and Saint Patrick's Cathedral in the Irish capital city of Dublin.

• Since 1962, the city of Chicago has dyed its river green as part of the Saint Patrick's Day fun!

Want to Know More?

In the Library

Kroll, Steven. *Mary McLean and the Saint Patrick's Day Parade*. New York: Scholastic, 1991.

MacGill-Callahan, Sheila. *The Last Snake in Ireland—A Story about Saint Patrick*. New York: Holiday House, 1999.

Schertle, Alice. *Jeremy Bean's Saint Patrick's Day*. New York: Lothrop, Lee, & Shepherd, 1987.

On the Web

Saint Patrick's Day

http://www.marvelicious.com/stpatrick.html

To hear Irish music, read Irish poems, and learn more about shamrocks and leprechauns

The History of Saint Patrick's Day

http://www.historychannel.com/exhibits/stpatricksday/

To learn more about the life of Saint Patrick, the holiday, and the history of Ireland and Irish-Americans

Through the Mail

Shamrock Station

Postmaster

Ireland, WV 26376

To have Saint Patrick's Day mail marked with a special "Shamrock Station" postmark, send stamped, addressed envelopes to this West Virginia Post Office. Include a note asking postal workers to do this.

On the Road

Saint Patrick's Cathedral

14 East 51st Street

New York, NY 10022

212/753-2261

To see the largest church of its style in the United States

Index

About the Author

Natalie M. Rosinsky writes about history, science, and other fun things. One of her two cats usually sits on her computer as she works in Mankato, Minnesota. Both cats pay close attention as she and her family make and eat special holiday foods. Natalie earned graduate degrees from the University of Wisconsin and has been a high school and college teacher.